A gift for:

From:

T0124068

Other books in this series:
The Secrets of Happiness 365   For my Mother 365   Inspiration 365
Words to live by... 365   365 Happy Days!   Our Planet 365

Other books by Helen Exley:
The little book of Happiness   Calm & Mindfulness   For my Friend
The book of Positive Thoughts   The little book of Smiles   Be You!

Published in 2011 and 2021 by Helen Exley ®LONDON in Great Britain.
Illustrated by Juliette Clarke © Helen Exley Creative Ltd 2011, 2021.
Selection and arrangement by Helen Exley © Helen Exley Creative Ltd 2011, 2021.

ISBN: 978-1-84634-498-5

12 11 10 9 8 7 6 5 4 3 2 1

Acknowledgements: The publishers are grateful for permission to reproduce copyright material.
Whilst every effort has been made to trace copyright holders, we would be pleased to hear from any not here acknowledged.

IMPORTANT COPYRIGHT NOTICE: Richard Alan, Rosanne Ambrose-Brown, Pam Brown, Pamela Dugdale, Helen Exley, Linda Macfarlane, Helen M. Exley, Marion C. Garretty, Susanta Ghosh, Stuart And Linda Macfarlane, Ingeborg Nelson, Priya Patel, Pushpa Patel, Helen Fitzwalter-Read, Jane Swan, Helen Thomson, Margot Thomson and Jenny De Vries are all © Helen Exley 2011, 2021.

Helen Exley ®LONDON, 16 Chalk Hill, Watford, Herts WD19 4BG, UK
www.helenexley.com

January 1

Two people, yes, two lasting friends.
The giving comes, the taking ends.
There is no measure for such things.
For this all Nature slows and sings.

ELIZABETH JENNINGS (1926-2001)

WHAT IS A HELEN EXLEY GIFTBOOK?

Helen Exley Giftbooks cover the most powerful relationships:
the love between couples, and the bonds within families or
between friends. A very strong theme in Helen's recent books
has been that of friendship and enduring relationships. Her team
of researchers spare no expense in making sure each book is as
thoughtful and meaningful as it is possible to create; good to give
and good to receive. You have the result in your hands.
If you find the quotes in *Friendship 365* helpful, please tell others.
There is no power like word-of-mouth recommendation.

January 2

A friend hears
the song in my heart and sings
it to me when my memory fails.

PIONEER GIRLS LEADERS' HANDBOOK

December 31

Glad till the dancing stops, and the lilt of the music ends. Laugh till the game is played; and be you merry my friends.

JOHN MASEFIELD (1878-1967)

January 3

From quiet homes
and first beginning,
Out to the undiscovered ends,
There's nothing worth
the wear of winning,
But laughter and the love of friends.

HILAIRE BELLOC (1870-1953)

December 30

Friendship is
the shadow of
the evening which
strengthens
with the setting sun
of life.

JEAN DE LA FONTAINE

January 4

A friend is one who knows
all about you
and loves you just the same.

ENTRY IN AN AUTOGRAPH ALBUM

December 29

I count your friendship
one of the chief pleasures of
my life, a comfort in time
of doubt and trouble,
a joy in time of prosperity
and success, and an
inspiration at all times.

EDWIN O. GROVER

January 5

B efore a friend I may think aloud.

RALPH WALDO EMERSON (1803-1882)

December 28

All we can do
is to make the best
of our friends,
love and cherish
what is good in them.

THOMAS JEFFERSON (1743-1826)

Happiness seems made to be shared.

JEAN RACINE (1639-1699)

December 27

W e feel more deeply,
remember more clearly,
enjoy events with greater
pleasure if we have a
friend to share with.

PAM BROWN

Oh dear! How unfortunate
I am not to have anyone to weep with!

MADAME DE SÉVIGNÉ (1626-1696)

December26

You're a real friend... anything I have I'd give to you. But nothing could pay you back for making me feel so special.

HELEN THOMSON

January 8

A true friend laughs at your stories
even when they're not so good,
and sympathizes with your troubles even
when they're not so bad.

PROVERB

Friendships are born out of trust,
shared values and little acts of kindness.

STUART AND LINDA MACFARLANE

January 9

Very few burdens are heavy
when everyone lifts.

AUTHOR UNKNOWN

December 24

For all your unconditional love, joy, enthusiasm, and for all you've given me this year, as my friend and my stalwart support – thank you.

PAM GILLON

January 10

Friendship can only
be measured
in memories, laughter,
peace and love.

STUART AND LINDA MACFARLANE

December 23

Be slow in choosing a friend,
slower in changing.

BENJAMIN FRANKLIN (1706-1790)

January 11

...if the mutual love of friends were
to be removed from the world, there is no
single house, no single state that would
go on existing; even agriculture would
cease to be.

CICERO (106-43 B.C.)

December 22

That's how it is with people sometimes.
When you least expect it,
a common thread begins to weave
together the fabric of friendship.

MARY KAY SHANLEY

Two people holding each other up like flying buttresses. Two people depending on each other and babying each other and defending each other against the world outside.

ERICA JONG, B.1942

December 21

With every true friendship we build more firmly the foundations on which the peace of the whole world rests.

MAHATMA GANDHI (1869-1948)

January 13

A friend is the person to whom
you'll open the door
when it's a bad hair day,
when you have chicken pox,
when you've just flooded
the kitchen, when the cat's used
his box enthusiastically.

PAM BROWN

December 20

Since there is nothing so well worth having as friends, never lose a chance to make them. For people are brought into constant contact with one another, and friends help and foes hinder at times and places where you least expect it.

FRANCESCO GUICCIADINI

January 14

Friends are probably the most important thing in life apart from family. I have four, probably more, whom I could ring up at three a.m. and say "I'm desperate, please come", and they would.

CLARE FRANCIS

December 19

A friend leaves a pie on the kitchen table,
a vase of fresh flowers by the bed –
and a note to welcome you home.

PAM BROWN

The bird a nest, the spider a web,
the person friendship.

WILLIAM BLAKE (1757-1827),
FROM "THE MARRIAGE OF HEAVEN AND HELL"

December 18

Life is nothing without friendship.

CICERO (106-43 B.C.)

January 16

You will find that if you share your friend's burden, both of you will walk a little straighter.

AUTHOR UNKNOWN,
FROM "SHARE THE HOPE"

December 17

There are red-letter days in our lives
when we meet people who thrill us like
a fine poem, people whose handshake
is brimful of unspoken sympathy and
whose sweet, rich natures impart
to our eager, impatient spirits
a wonderful restfulness...

HELEN KELLER (1880-1968)

January 17

"This I must remember to describe",
"I wish that they were here to share
this view, this meal, this small adventure."

PAMELA DUGDALE

December 16

When friendship deserts us we are lonely and helpless as a ship, left by the high tide upon the shore. When friendship returns to us, it is as though the tide came back, gave us buoyancy and freedom, and opened to us the wide places of the world.

HARRY EMERSON FOSDICK (1878-1969)

January 18

My friend:
Who hears me,
who understands me,
becomes mine...
for all time.

RALPH WALDO EMERSON
(1803-1882)

December 15

Thank you for believing in me – even when I doubted myself.

HELEN FITZWALTER-READ

January 19

You're the only person who is always there when I need someone to tell just how hard-done-by I am. And somehow, without saying a thing, you help me realize just how strong I am.

HELEN THOMSON

December 14

The ornament
of a house is the friends
who frequent it.

RALPH WALDO EMERSON
(1803-1882)

January 20

I with you, and you with me,
Miles are short with company.

GEORGE ELIOT [MARY ANN EVANS]
(1819-1880)

December 13

I have always made
a distinction between my
friends and my confidants.
I enjoy the conversation
of the former; from
the latter I hide nothing.

EDITH PIAF (1915-1963)

January 21

The weary miles pass swiftly,
taken in a joyous stride.
And all the world seems
brighter, when a friend
walks by our side.

AUTHOR UNKNOWN

December 12

What a blessing a realistic friend can be. When temptation rears its head she'll always say "Look at the price tag!"

PAM BROWN

January 22

The greatest healing therapy
is friendship and love.

HUBERT HUMPHREY (1911-1978)

December 11

No one is the whole of themselves;
their friends are the rest of them.

HARRY EMERSON FOSDICK (1878-1969)

January 23

A good friend is someone
who forgives you as soon
as you apologise.
A great friend is one who forgives
you before you apologise.

STUART AND LINDA MACFARLANE

December 10

My friend didn't feel sorry for me. She believed that I had the strength within me to recover and to grow. That was the kindest thing she could have done. That was her great gift.

HELEN THOMSON

January24

How life catches up with us
and teaches us to love and forgive
each other.

JUDY COLLINS, B.1939

Two may talk together under the same
roof for many years,
yet never really meet; and two others
at first speech are old friends.

MARY CATHERWOOD (1847-1901)

January 25

Friendship, then, both adds
a brighter radiance to prosperity
and relieves adversity by dividing
and sharing the burden.

CICERO (106-43 B.C.)

December 8

A blessed thing it is for any man or woman to have a friend; one human soul whom we can trust utterly; who knows the best and the worst of us, and who loves us in spite of all our faults; who will speak the honest truth to us, while the world flatters us to our face, and laughs behind our back.

CHARLES KINGSLEY (1819-1875)

A friend is the only one
allowed to say "I told you so."

PAM BROWN

December 7

F riendship
without self-interest
is one of the rare
and beautiful things
of life.

JAMES BYRNES

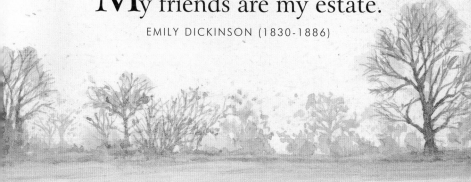

My friends are my estate.

EMILY DICKINSON (1830-1886)

December 6

Some people come into our lives
and quickly go...
Some people stay for a while
and leave their footprints on our
hearts, and we are never,
ever the same.

FLAVIA

January 28

If the while I think on thee,
dear friend,
All losses are restored,
and sorrows end.

WILLIAM SHAKESPEARE (1564-1616)

December 5

Friendship is...
temperate and equal,
a constant established
heat, all gentle and smooth,
without poignancy
or roughness.

MICHEL EYQUEM DE MONTAIGNE
(1533-1592)

January 29

It's all the little understandings,
the unnoticed kindlinesses, the hundreds
of gentlest smiles... it's dozens of little
acts of friendship that have made my life.

HELEN THOMSON

December 4

There is no friend like the old friend
who has shared our morning days.
No greeting like their welcome,
no homage like their praise.

OLIVER WENDELL HOLMES
(1809-1894)

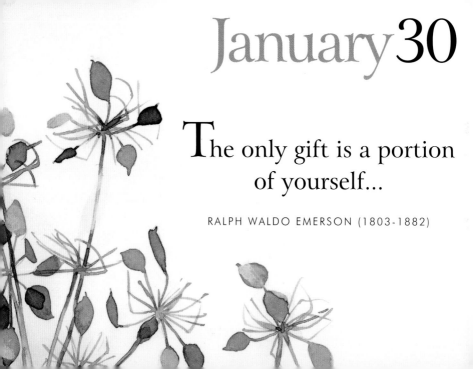

January 30

The only gift is a portion
of yourself...

RALPH WALDO EMERSON (1803-1882)

December 3

My fellow, my companion,
held most dear.
My soul, my other self, my
inward friend

MARY SIDNEY HERBERT

January 31

It is not that a person has occasion often to fall back upon the kindness of friends; perhaps we may never experience the necessity of doing so; but we are governed by our imaginations, and they stand there as a solid and impregnable bulwark against all the evils of life.

SYDNEY SMITH (1771-1845)

December 2

When I dig a hole for myself and sit at the bottom and gloom – whose face peers over the edge and calls down, "Tea and cookies!?" Yours, of course.

PAM BROWN

February 1

With a person I trust
I can tell her all my
problems without anyone
knowing. I can tell her
all my secrets
like a secret diary.

PRIYA PATEL, AGE 10

December 1

A faithful friend... will rejoice
at your prosperity and grieve at your
adversity, will bear half of your burden –
will add to your joys,
and diminish your sorrows by
sharing in both.

JAMES GIBBONS (1834-1921)

February 2

First of all things, for friendship, there must be that delightful, indefinable state called feeling at ease with your companion, the one man, the one woman out of a multitude who interests you, who meets your thoughts and tastes.

JULIA DUHRING

November 30

One does not
make friends;
one recognizes them.

ISABEL PATERSON

A friend is a person with whom
I may be sincere.

RALPH WALDO EMERSON (1803-1882)

November 29

W hen the spirits sink too low,
the best cordial is to read over all
the letters of one's friends.

WILLIAM SHENSTONE (1714-1763)

February 4

The shared memories brought
smiles, laughter,
a few tears and, at last, a sense
of contentment.

MARY KAY SHANLEY

November 28

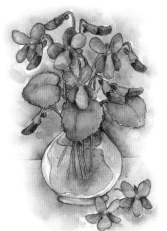

If you want an accounting of your worth, count your friends.

MARY BROWNE

February5

Friendship or the capacity
for it is a gift.

MARY O'HARA, FROM "CELEBRATION OF LOVE"

November 27

We are not primarily put on the earth
to see through one another,
but to see one another through.

PETER DE VRIES

February 6

Forgiving is a huge act of kindness.
It says, "I understand", "I care", and
"I am your friend".

STUART AND LINDA MACFARLANE

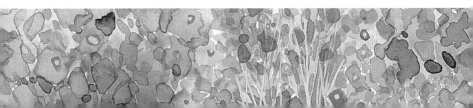

November 26

What would I do without
a friend like you?
– someone to say, sometimes,
Just Forget The Expense!
Just Forget The Diet!
Just Forget What People
Think!

PAM BROWN

February 7

"I'll be right there" is the best promise a friend makes.

HELEN THOMSON

November 25

May the road rise to meet you.
May the wind be always at your back, the sun
shine warm upon your face, the rain fall soft
upon your fields...

IRISH TOAST

February 8

I never crossed
your threshold with a grief,
but that I went without it.

THEODOSIA GARRISON (1874-1944)

November 24

Deft thieves can break your
locks and carry off your savings,
fire consume your home...
Fortune can't take away what you
give to friends: that wealth stays
yours forever.

MARCUS MARTIAL (C.40-104 A.D.)

February 9

There is a wonderful, mystical law of nature that the three things we crave most in life – happiness, freedom, and peace of mind – are always attained by giving them to someone else.

AUTHOR UNKNOWN

November 23

In a thousand ways my friends
have turned my limitations into
beautiful privileges,
and enabled me to walk serene
and happy in the shadow cast
by my deprivation.

HELEN KELLER (1880-1968)

Who shall explain the extraordinary instinct that tells us, perhaps after a single meeting, that this or that particular person in some mysterious way matters to us?

ARTHUR CHRISTOPHER BENSON
(1862-1925)

Don't be dismayed at goodbyes.
A farewell is necessary before you can meet
again. And meeting again, after moments
or lifetimes, is certain for those
who are friends.

RICHARD BACH

February 11

A friend in need is a friend indeed.

PROVERB

November 21

My best friend is the one who brings
out the best in me.

HENRY FORD (1863-1947)

February 12

The good thing about friends
is not having to finish sentences.

BRIAN JONES

November 20

When friends stop being frank and useful to each other, the whole world loses some of its radiance.

ANATOLE BROYARD (1920-1990)

February 13

The last time I saw you, I told myself:
I would see nothing, ever again;
and the evening stars that fell to earth
can make the distance between us
no shorter.

JAYANTA MAHAPATRA,
FROM "BONE OF TIME"

November 19

I love tranquil solitude
And such society
As is quiet, wise and good.

PERCY BYSSHE SHELLEY (1792-1822)

February 14

The happiness of life is made up of minute fractions – the little, soon-forgotten charities of a kiss, a smile, a kind look, a heartfelt compliment... and the countless other infinitesimals of pleasant thought and feeling.

SAMUEL TAYLOR COLERIDGE (1772-1834)

November 18

Throughout all eternity – including now – the deep respect and trust of a friend is probably the most satisfying of life's experiences.

WALTER MACPEEK

February 15

When I thought that the phone would never ring again, you sensed my loneliness. And I learned that the most happy-making words in the world were –
"Hi! It's me!"

CHRISTINE HARRIS

November 17

What a wretched lot of old shrivelled creatures we shall be by-and-by. Never mind – the uglier we get in the eyes of others, the lovelier we shall be to each other; that has always been my firm faith about friendship...

GEORGE ELIOT [MARY ANN EVANS](1819-1880)

February 16

The glory of friendship is not the outstretched hand, nor the kindly smile nor the joy of companionship; it is the spirited inspiration that comes to you when you discover that someone else believes in you and is willing to trust you with their friendship.

RALPH WALDO EMERSON (1803-1882)

November 16

We may exasperate each other
sometimes but we are friends always.

PAM BROWN

February 17

When despair strikes –
only a friend,
a tub of ice cream
can sooth the soul.

PAM BROWN

November 15

Yet "old friends" always seemed
a contradiction to me. Age cannot wither
nor custom stale the infinite variety of friends
who, as long as you know them,
remain as vibrant and stimulating
as the day you first met them.

AUTHOR UNKNOWN

February 18

...the finest thing of all about friendship
is that it sends a ray of good hope into
the future, and keeps us from faltering
or falling to the wayside.

CICERO (106-43 B.C.)

November 14

Friendship is fit for serene days,
and graceful gifts, and country rambles,
but also for rough roads and hard fare,
shipwreck, poverty, and persecution.

RALPH WALDO EMERSON (1803-1882)

February 19

Like the shade
of a great tree in the
noonday heat is a friend.
Like the home port with
your country's flag flying
after a long journey is
a friend.

AUTHOR UNKNOWN

November 13

Robbing life of friendship is like robbing the world of the sun.

CICERO (106-43 B.C.)

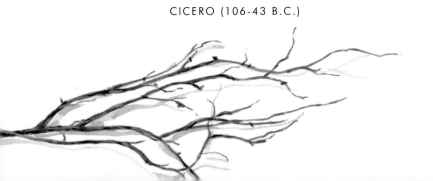

February 20

Silences and distances are woven
into the texture of every true friendship.

ROBERTA ISRAELOFF

November 12

A friend will give you
good advice – and stand by you
when you ignore it.

PAMELA DUGDALE

February 21

I think there is, in friendship,
an instant recognition –
a kind of loving. It needs just a word,
the touch of a hand.

HELEN M. EXLEY

November 11

One of the most beautiful
qualities of true friendship
is to understand
and to be understood.

SENECA (C. 4-65 A.D.)

February 22

W ith a friend at your side,
no road seems too long.

JAPANESE PROVERB

November 10

Love comes from blindness.
Friendship comes from knowledge.

COMTE DE BUSSY-RABUTIN (1618-1693)

Since everything that is mortal is
precarious and transient,
we ought always to go on and on
searching for people who can
receive our love and be loved
by us in return.

LAELIUS

November 9

We cannot tell the precise moment when friendship is formed. As in filling a vessel drop by drop, there is at last a drop which makes it run over, so in a series of kindnesses there is at last one that makes the heart run over.

DR. SAMUEL JOHNSON (1709-1784), QUOTED BY JAMES BOSWELL

February 24

Friendships are the places where
we gossip, enjoy, explore and feel at ease
with people who are similar to us and
care about us.

ROSALYN CHISSICK

November 8

Thank you for making me feel fun, noticed, important. What more could I ask!

HELEN THOMSON

A friend means it
when after twenty years apart
she says you haven't changed.

PAM BROWN

November 7

Only friends will tell you
the truths you need to hear to make...
your life bearable.

FRANÇINE DU PLESSIX GRAY (1930-2019)

February 26

My coat and I live comfortably together. It has assumed all my wrinkles, does not hurt me anywhere, has moulded itself on my deformities, and is complacent to all my movements... Old coats and old friends are the same thing.

VICTOR HUGO (1802-1885)

November 6

Will you be my friend,
my friend of friends,
beyond everyone,
everything, forever and
forever?

HENRY JAMES (1843-1916)

February 27

Thanks for being a friend,
a storyteller, a super cook,
a handy dressmaker,
a homework helper, a peacemaker,
an understanding person,
a television critic,
a shopping companion,
a joke-sharer or, in other words,
a perfect saint!

ORLA MAGUIRE, AGE 11

November 5

With good friends
and good food on board,
and good wine in the pitcher,
we may well ask,
when shall we live if not now?

M.F.K. FISHER, FROM "THE ART OF EATING"

February 28/29

True happiness consists
not in the multitude of friends,
but in their worth and choice.

BEN JONSON (1572-1637)

November 4

Not anybody and everybody can be your friend. It must be someone as close to you as your skin, someone who imparts color, drama, meaning to your life.

HENRY MILLER (1891-1980)

March 1

A constant friend
is rare and hard to find.

PLUTARCH

November 3

W hat a mercy it is
that friends don't notice
that either of you are getting older.

PAM BROWN

MY FRIEND

My friend is like bark rounding a tree
who warms like sun on a winter day and cools
like water in the hot noon.
He is my friend and I am his.

EMILY HEARN, FROM "HOCKEY CARDS AND HOPSCOTCH"

November2

Friendship needs no words –
it is solitude delivered from the anguish
of loneliness.

DAG HAMMERSKJÖLD (1905-1961)

March 3

Anything, everything,
little or big becomes
an adventure when the right
person shares it.

KATHLEEN NORRIS (1880-1966)

November 1

The friends who listen to us are the ones we move toward, and we want to sit in their radius. When we are listened to, it creates us, makes us unfold and expand.

KARL MENNINGER

March 4

A friend is an impregnable citadel of refuge in the strife of existence. It is your friend that keeps your faith in human nature, that makes you believe that it is a good universe.

AUTHOR UNKNOWN

October 31

It is a good thing to be rich,
and a good thing to be strong,
but it is a better thing to be loved
of many friends.

EURIPIDES (C.485-406 B.C.)

March 5

One needs different
people in one's life...
A harbour in which to seek
shelter against the storm,
or simply to pay
a visit because it is such
a beautiful day.

K. DEPOORTERE

October 30

Life is not made up of great sacrifices
and duties, but of little things;
in which smiles and kindness given
habitually are what win and preserve
the heart and secure comfort.

SIR HUMPHRY DAVY (1778-1829)

March 6

Although far apart, friends are still linked by a common bond of affection as if a path through the ether exists between them.

STUART AND LINDA MACFARLANE

I want to be your friend
Forever and ever without break
or decay.
When the hills are all flat
And the rivers are all dry,
Not till then will I part from you.

CHINESE OATH OF FRIENDSHIP, 1ST CENTURY

March 7

Without affection
and kindly feeling life
can hold no joys.

CICERO (106-43 B.C.)

October 28

Kindness makes the difference
between passion and caring.
Kindness is tenderness, kindness
is love, perhaps greater than love...
kindness is goodwill, kindness says
"I want you to be happy."

RANDOLPH RAY

March 8

A girl friend is the one person
with whom you don't have to
be clever or sophisticated
or adult or responsible.

PAM BROWN

We take care of our health, we lay up money, we make our roof tight and our clothing sufficient, but who provides wisely that he shall not be wanting in the best property of all – friends.

RALPH WALDO EMERSON (1803-1882)

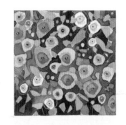

Friendship is a sheltering tree.

SAMUEL TAYLOR COLERIDGE (1772-1834)

On the outskirts of Havana,
they call friends *mi tierra*,
my country, or *mi sangre*,
my blood. In Caracas,
a friend is *mi pana*, my bread,
or *mi llave*, my key.

EDUARDO GALEANO, B.1940,
FROM "THE BOOK OF EMBRACES"

Friends have something you lack, like optimism. They make you feel everything is going to be all right with the world as long as they are around.

BESSIE HEAD (1937-1986)

October25

A friend takes
all your miseries and
reshapes them
into hope.

PAM BROWN

March 11

You need to be able to confide,
to laugh together.
It's just about as important as breathing.

ROSAMUNDE PILCHER (1924-2019)

October24

It is a mistake to think that one makes
a friend because of his or her qualities,
it has nothing to do with qualities at
all. It is the person that we want,
not what he does or says, or does
not do or say, but what he is that is
eternally enough!

ARTHUR CHRISTOPHER BENSON (1862-1925)

That's what friendship's really about – someone who can uncrumble you when you collapse, and someone who lifts you up higher when you're high.

HELEN THOMSON

October 23

She notices when I'm tired or sickening for flu before I do. She's tuned into me so that she can give me loads of advice – sometimes very unwelcome, when it arrives before I'm ready for it.

JENNY DE VRIES

Friendships are our lifelines
and our support system.

BROOKE SHIELDS, B.1965

October 22

A life without friendship;
a sky without stars.

CHRISTINE HARRIS

March 14

No life is so strong and complete
But it yearns for the smile of a friend.

WALLACE BRUCE

October 21

Life is to be fortified by many friendships. To love, and to be loved, is the greatest happiness of existence.

SYDNEY SMITH (1771-1845)

March 15

Who is more indefatigable in
toil, when there is occasion
for toil, than a friend?
Who is readier to rejoice in
one's good fortune?
Whose praise is sweeter?

SAINT JOHN CHRYSOSTOM (C.345-407 A.D.)

October 20

Without friends,
the world is
but a wilderness.

ANONYMOUS

March 16

There are friendships that last
only a moment.
But a word or gesture can change a life,
be cherished forever, give solace,
bring hope in darkness
And endure for a lifetime.

PAMELA DUGDALE

October 19

We rejoice in the joys of our friends as much as we do our own, and we are equally grieved at their sorrows. And whatever labour he would encounter with a view to his own pleasure, he will encounter also for the sake of his friend.

CICERO (106-43 B.C.)

March 17

I know now that the world is not filled with strangers. It is full of other people – waiting only to be spoken to.

BETH DAY

October 18

Lost friendships. Lost loves.
And yet they've never been forgotten.

PAM BROWN

March 18

Here's to all the little things,
the "done-and-then-forgotten" things,
Those "oh-it's-simply-nothing" things
That make life worth the fight.

AUTHOR UNKNOWN

We want two or three friends,
but these we cannot do without,
and they serve us
in every thought we think.

RALPH WALDO EMERSON (1803-1882)

March 19

W hat's friendship realest measure?...
The amount of precious time you'll
squander on someone else's calamities...

RICHARD FORD, B.1944

October 16

Books and friends
should be few but good.

PROVERB

March 20

A friend like you isn't for Emergencies only – but for small, cheerful jaunts and jollifications and everyday comfort.

PAM BROWN

October 15

Much of the pleasure in doing something new comes from the thought of telling a friend all about it.

LINDA MACFARLANE, B.1953

March 21

Friends are together when they are separated, they are rich when they are poor, strong when they are weak, and – a thing even harder to explain – they live on after they have died.

CICERO (106-43 B.C.)

October 14

Money can buy many things,
good and evil. All the wealth of the world
could not buy you a friend or pay you
for the loss of one.

G.D. PRENTICE

One lonely person
one other lonely person
one shy smile
one friendly grin
two happy people

HELEN EXLEY

A friend carries a list of books
you are searching for.
And you have hers.

PAMELA DUGDALE

March 23

I love you for putting your hand into my heaped-up heart and passing over all the foolish and frivolous and weak things that you can't help dimly seeing there, and for drawing out into the light all the beautiful radiant belongings that no one else had looked quite far enough to find.

ROY CROFT

October 12

Constant use had not worn ragged
the fabric of their friendship.

F. PARKER

March 24

Though love be deeper,
friendship is more wide...

CORINNE ROOSEVELT ROBINSON

My world is made by my friends.

HELEN EXLEY

A man without friends
is like a left hand without a right.

SOLOMON IBN GABIROL
(1020-1070)

It is kindness in a person not beauty, which wins our love.

MARK ORTMAN

...while I retain your friendship
I retain the best that life
has given me next to that which
is the deepest and gravest joy
in all human experience.

GEORGE ELIOT [MARY ANN EVANS] (1819-1880)

October 9

You bring sunshine to my rainy day.

PROVERB

March 27

May the roof above us never fall in,
and may the friends
gathered below never fall out.

IRISH TOAST

October 8

A friend is the one who is putting their car away after a hard morning's shopping, sees you plodding up the road and gets it out again.

PAM BROWN

However rare true love may be,
it is less so than true friendship.

FRANCOIS, DUC DE LA ROCHEFOUCAULD (1613-1680)

October 7

We strive for glory, honour,
fame, but when we near
the end of life
we find that happiness
depends on none of these,
but love of friends.

AUTHOR UNKNOWN

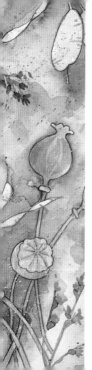

March 29

A friend like you
is an old and well worn
dressing-gown to wrap around me
when the world seems
dark and cold.

PAM BROWN

October 6

True friends, like ivy and the wall
Both stand together, and together fall.

FRANCIS BACON (1561-1626)

...one of the qualities I value most in a friend is discretion. You must be able to know that you can be absolutely frank with the person you are talking to. The privilege of confidence binds people together, as does the mutual vulnerability it implies.

ROBIN COOK (1946-2005)

October 5

Before borrowing money
from a friend,
decide which you need most.

W.A. CLARKE

There's nothing more precious in this world than the feeling of being wanted.

DIANA DORS (1931-1984)

October 4

One can do without people,
but one has need of a friend.

CHINESE PROVERB

April 1

When friends meet, hearts warm.

PROVERB

October 3

Friendships shape the course of our lives, leading us through thicket, struggling across burns, scrambling up hillsides and clambering over dales. A tiring journey but the company is good.

STUART AND LINDA MACFARLANE

Parting is loss
and the tiny ache of regret
stays with us always.

HELEN M. EXLEY

When two people are at one in their inmost hearts, they shatter even the strength of iron or bronze. And when two people understand each other in their inmost hearts, their words are sweet and strong, like the fragrance of orchids.

THE I CHING

April 3

A friend takes you on, warts and all.

RICHARD ALAN

October 1

At every stage
of my life friendship
has been the main
source of my quite
outrageously enjoyable
existence.

SIR GEOFFREY KEYNES

I am arrived at last in
the presence of someone so real
and equal, that I may drop even
those undermost garments
of dissimulation, courtesy,
and second thought,
which we never put off...

RALPH WALDO EMERSON (1803-1882)

September 30

Friendship is sincere.
It scorns flattery. It faces facts.
It is a lift...
It is not a thing to be hurried.

R.L. JONES

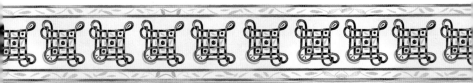

April 5

No matter where we are we need those friends who trudge across from their neighbourhoods to ours.

STEPHEN PETERS

Wherever you are it is your own friends who make your world.

WILLIAM JAMES (1842-1910)

Why do people lament their follies
for which their friends adore them?

GERARD MANLEY HOPKINS (1844-1889)

September 28

You're the best there is.
What a privilege it is to know you.

LISA SCULLY-O'GRADY

My brightest spot...
is the deliciously calm new friendship
that Herbert Spencer gives me.
We see each other every day, and have
a delightful camaraderie in everything.
But for him my life
would be desolate enough.

GEORGE ELIOT [MARY ANN EVANS] (1819-1880)

September 27

The Beatles knew what they were about when they wrote their song, "I'll get by with a little help from my friends". How else would any of us get by without this stretching out of hands to friends, neighbours, nations?

KAY DICK, FROM " FRIENDS AND FRIENDSHIP"

The test of friendship is assistance in adversity, and that, too, unconditional assistance.

MAHATMA GANDHI (1869-1948)

You were always there.
No one else was.

HELEN EXLEY

Friends, companions, lovers,
are those who treat us
in terms of our unlimited worth
to ourselves.

HENRY ALONZO MYERS

September 25

A friend knows how to allow for mere quantity in your talk, and only replies to the quality...

WILLIAM DEAN HOWELLS (1837-1920)

What's the fun
of an adventure
if you can't share it
with a friend?

PAM BROWN

September 24

Friendship! Sweetener of life!
And solder of society!

ROBERT BLAIR (1699-1747)

April 11

Love is blind; friendship
closes its eyes.

PROVERB

September 23

...I wait for you, I even urge on you to come; for I have anxieties, many pressing cares, of which I think, if I had once had your ears to listen to me, I could unburden myself in the conversation of a single walk.

CICERO (106-43 B.C.),
IN A LETTER TO HIS FRIEND, ATTICUS

April 12

For taking the time to listen – thank you.

STUART AND LINDA MACFARLANE

September 22

Old friends are best.
King James used to call for his old shoes;
they were easiest for his feet.

JOHN SELDEN (1584-1654)

April 13

...there can be no happiness
equal to the joy of finding a person
that understands.

VICTOR ROBINSON

September 21

I would rather have your friendship than: win the lottery, become a famous rock musician, discover a new planet, find the secret of eternal youth, have a whole bag of jelly babies all to myself.

STUART AND LINDA MACFARLANE

April 14

No good thing is pleasant to possess, without friends to share it.

SENECA (C.4-65 A.D.)

September 20

We take our friends with us
wherever we go – and say to ourselves:
"They would love this".

PAM BROWN

Happy is the house that shelters a friend!

RALPH WALDO EMERSON (1803-1882)

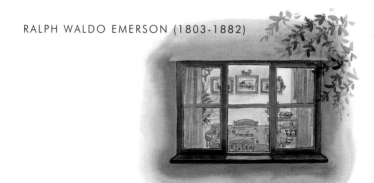

September 19

I count myself in nothing else
so happy As in a soul remembering
my good friends.

WILLIAM SHAKESPEARE (1564-1616),
FROM "KING RICHARD II"

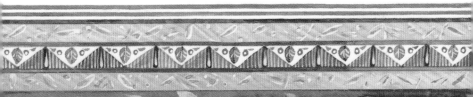

In friendship we find nothing false or insincere; everything is straightforward.

CICERO (106-43 B.C.)

September 18

When I see my friend
I feel the joy deep inside
me, like a pilgrim
who is lost and finds
the right way at last.

G. LAENEN

Friendship bears all things,
believes all things,
hopes all things,
endures all things.

Friendship never ends.

ADAPTED FROM 1 CORINTHIANS 1

September 17

How often have we built each other as shelters against the cold.

AUDRE LORDE (1934-1992)

April 18

May friendship, like wine, improve
as time advances,
And may we always have old wine, old
friends, and young cares.

AUTHOR UNKNOWN

September 16

It is easy to say how we love
new friends, and what we think of them,
but words can never trace out
all the fibres that knit us to the old.

GEORGE ELIOT [MARY ANN EVANS] (1819-1880)

Littlest kindnesses repeated a thousand times have the greatest value.

PUSHPA PATEL

September 15

When a goose gets sick or wounded or shot down, two geese drop out of the formation and follow her down to help and protect her. They stay with her until she is either able to fly again or dies. Then they start out again, either joining another formation or catching up with the original flock.

AUTHOR UNKNOWN

April 20

After breathing and eating and sleeping, friendships are essential to our survival.

ADELAIDE BRY

September 14

A friend accepts you
for who you are,
but expects you to be all
you can be.

RICHARD LOUV, FROM "THE WEB OF LIFE"

April 21

The world is very small.
A tiny raft afloat in a sea of stars.
Friendship is not a choice
but a necessity if we are not
to capsize.

PAMELA DUGDALE

September 13

Love... respect... loyalty... that, surely,
is what true friendship is all about.

TARA MCKENZIE

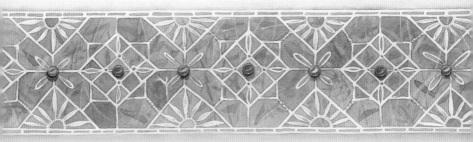

April 22

...when people have light in themselves, it will shine out from them. Then we get to know each other as we walk together in the darkness, without needing to pass our hands over each other's faces, or to intrude into each other's hearts.

ALBERT SCHWEITZER (1875-1965)

September 12

What can give us more joy
than a friend? Even more, is there
something we need more?

DESIDERIUS ERASMUS (c.1466-1536)

I awoke this morning with devout
thanksgiving for my friends, the old
and the new.

RALPH WALDO EMERSON (1803-1882)

September 11

Thus nature has no love
for solitude, and always leans,
as it were, on some support;
and the sweetest support is found
in the most intimate friendship.

CICERO (106-43 B.C.)

I hope you find joy
in the great things of life –
but also in the little things.
A flower, a song,
a butterfly on your hand.

ELLEN LEVINE

September 10

My courage, my growing
strength and happiness.
I hope they've been
the best thank-you
I could have given you.

HELEN EXLEY

April 25

Friends: one is not happy without the other, nor can either of them be miserable alone. As if they could change bodies, they take their turns in pain as well as in pleasure; relieving one another in their most adverse conditions.

WILLIAM PENN (1644-1718)

September 9

We have been friends so long.
Thank you for your constancy
and all the kindness
that has made you dear to me.

PAM BROWN

Happiness is my friend's hand.

GILLIAN QUEEN, AGE 10

September 8

I don't want to be near you for
the thoughts we share but the words
we never have to speak.

NIKKI GIOVANNI

It's the song ye sing,
and the smiles ye wear,
That's a makin' the sun shine
everywhere.

JAMES WHITCOMB RILEY (1849-1916)

September 7

It is in the multitude of little,
everyday things, kind words, letters
to keep in touch, surprise gifts,
and the willingness to listen,
that the ordinary person gets the
opportunity to become a friend.

STUART AND LINDA MACFARLANE

April 28

A friend is the person
to whom you'll open
the door when
nobody else will do.

PAM BROWN

September 6

If you have
one true friend
you have more
than your share.

THOMAS FULLER
(1608-1661)

Friendship is a word
the very sight of which
in print makes
the heart warm.

AUGUSTINE BIRRELL (1850-1933)

September 5

My Friend.
In prosperity our friends
know us;
In adversity we know our friends.

SIR JAMES M. BARRIE (1860-1937)

April 30

This poem goes on too long because our friendship has been long, long for this life and these times, long as art is long and uninterruptable, and I would make it as long as I hope our friendship lasts if I could make poems that long.

FRANK O'HARA

September 4

For the loftiest friendships
have no commercial element
in them; to the contrary,
they are founded on sacrifice.
They neither expect nor
desire gift for gift or service
for service.

SARAH B. COOPER

May 1

A road to a friend's house is never long.

DANISH PROVERB

September 3

True blue friends... make you feel good and warm; they are automatically on the same wavelength; you can speak freely to them, you don't have to be on guard; they really listen; they care about what you're doing...

ADELAIDE BRY

May 2

If the friend is close at hand,
that is best; but if she is far away
she still is there to think of, to
wonder about, to hear from,
to write to, to share life and
experience with, to serve,
to honour, to admire, to love.

ARTHUR CHRISTOPHER BENSON (1862-1925)

September 2

Don't walk in front of me,
I may not follow.
Don't walk behind me,
I may not lead.
Walk beside me,
And just be my friend.

ALBERT CAMUS (1913-1960)

May 3

We all love best not those who offend us least, nor those who have done most for us, but those who make it most easy for us to forgive them.

SAMUEL BUTLER (1835-1902)

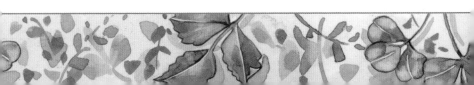

September 1

Only solitary people know
the full joys of friendship.
Others have their family;
but to a solitary and an exile
friends are everything.

WILLA CATHER (1873-1947)

May 4

If I don't have friends,
then I ain't got nothin'.

BILLIE HOLIDAY (1915-1959)

August 31

A friend is the one who,
in dubious circumstances,
aids deeds when deeds
are necessary.

PLAUTUS, FROM "EPIDICUS"

When we can share –
that is poetry in the prose of life.

SIGMUND FREUD (1856-1939)

August 30

We need old friends to help us grow old and new friends to help us stay young.

LETTY COTTIN POGREBIN, B.1939

Best friend, my well-spring
in the wilderness!

GEORGE ELIOT [MARY ANN EVANS] (1819-1880)

August 29

One can afford to lose a great deal on this earth when the sun shines on it, and not feel any the worse for the loss: but a single shred of human affection, one can't afford to lose, – tho' the sun and moon and stars shone all at once!

ELIZABETH BARRETT TO MARY RUSSELL MITFORD

A true friend unbosoms freely, advises justly, assists readily, adventures boldly, takes ill patiently, defends courageously, and continues a friend unchangeably.

WILLIAM PENN (1644-1718)

Friendship, like home, is where we go
when nobody else will have us.

JULIE BURCHILL

Love is caviar and wedding cake,
strawberries and cream.
Love is champagne.
Friendship is new bread,
fresh butter, farmhouse cheese
and a pot of tea for two.

PAM BROWN

To meet an old friend in a distant land
is like refreshing rain after a drought.

CHINESE PROVERB

May 9

We do not mind our arriving anywhere nearly so much as our not having any company on the way.

FRANK MOORE COLBY

...friendship, the ease of it,
it is not something to be taken lightly –
nor for granted.

ADELAIDE BRY

But every road
is tough to me
That has no friend
to cheer it.

ELIZABETH SHANE

A night without a morning,
A trouble without end,
A life of bitter scorning,
A world without a friend.

JOHN CLARE (1793-1864)

May 11

I can take a criticism
from my friend
because I know she's
on my side.

HELEN THOMSON

August 24

A faithful friend is the elixir of life.

ECCLESIASTICUS 6:14-16

May 12

Friendship is by its very nature freer of deceit than any other relationship we can know because it is the bond least affected by striving for power, physical pleasure, or material profit, most liberated from any oath of duty or of constancy.

FRANCINE DU PLESSIX GRAY (B.1930-2019)

August 23

We who have friends
are wrapped around
in kindliness
and safe from the cold
immensity of space.

PAM BROWN

May 13

She is a friend of my mind.
She gathers me. The pieces I am,
she gathers them and gives them
back to me in all the right order.
It's good when you've got a woman
who is a friend of your mind.

TONI MORRISON

August 22

Our friendships are... the structures that hold us in place when our world threatens to dissolve.

ROSALYN CHISSICK,
FROM "NEW WOMAN",
AUGUST 1994

May 14

We need each other to share
the mysteries of life and death,
to give substance to our joy and sorrows,
to help us on our journey.

AUTHOR UNKNOWN

August 21

Friendship adds a brighter radiance
to prosperity and lightens the burden of
adversity by dividing and sharing it.

CICERO (106-43 B.C.)

Friendship is like the air
we breathe.
We take it for granted
yet need it to survive.

SUSANTA GHOSH

August 20

Then little by little we discover one friend, in the midst of the crowd of friends, who is particularly happy to be with us and to whom, we realize, we have an infinite number of things to say.

NATALIA GINZBURG (1916-1991),
FROM "THE LITTLE VIRTUES"

When they are real, friendships are not glass threads or frost-work, but the solidest thing we know.

RALPH WALDO EMERSON (1803-1882)

August 19

There are no goodbyes
for us. Wherever you are,
you will always be
in my heart.

MAHATMA GANDHI
(1869-1948)

May17

A fire gives warmth
and light,
and likewise a friend.

G. LAENEN

August 18

May the hinges of friendship never rust, or the wings of love lose a feather.

EDWARD BANNERMAN RAMSAY

May 18

I would have thought that tears
were the things which bound us together,
but no – smiles, laughter...

KATHARINE HEPBURN (1907-2003)

August 17

A real friend
is one who walks
in when the rest
of the world walks out.

ALBAN GOODIER (1869-1939)

May 19

I always felt that the great high privilege, relief and comfort of friendship was that one had to explain nothing.

KATHERINE MANSFIELD (1888-1923)

August 16

The visit of a friend
is medicine to the sick.

AUTHOR UNKNOWN

May 20

Thank you for knowing what needs doing, and doing it. Whether it's giving a hug, or a bandage, or a cup of tea. Or just knowing when to do nothing.

SARAH NELSON

August 15

I believe in friendship at first sight.

LINDA MACFARLANE, B.1953

May 21

Friendship is unnecessary,
like philosophy, like art...
It has no survival value;
rather it is one of those things
that gives value to survival.

C.S. LEWIS (1898-1963)

August 14

I want someone to laugh with me,
someone to be grave with me,
and at times, no doubt, to admire
my acuteness
and penetration.

ROBERT BURNS
(1759-1796)

We phone one another, write letters,
send each other postcards when we are away.
Signals to show each other we're not alone.
That someone cares.

ROSANNE AMBROSE-BROWN

The worst solitude is to be destitute of sincere friendship.

FRANCIS BACON (1561-1626)

May 23

One can bear grief,
but it takes two to be glad.

ELIZABETH HUBBARD

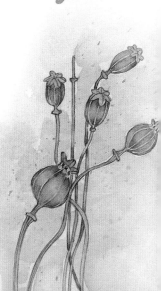

August 12

The making of friends,
who are real friends,
is the best token
we have of a person's
success in life.

EDWARD EVERETT HALE
(1822-1909)

I could sit here and list all the little things you do that deserve my gratitude. It would take yonks and it would bore you stiff. I guess that the best way to say "thank you" is to enjoy it all to the full and to love you rotten!

JENNY DE VRIES

August 11

The wealthiest of us is poor
and miserable, if we have no friend
whom we can grasp by the hand,
and to whom we can disclose
the secrets of our heart.

JAMES GIBBONS (1834-1921)

May25

Each contact
with a human being
is so rare,
so precious,
one should
preserve it.

ANAIS NIN (1903-1977)

August 10

Thank you to all the friends who wrap parcels for you when you're too busy, who never repeat what you said in that stupid outburst, who never borrow and then keep your books. They're the people who glue the world together!

HELEN THOMSON

In my friend,
I find a second self.

ISABEL NORTON

Friends are
all that matter.

GELETT BURGESS

May 27

A friend knows when to talk things through, but, most of all, a friend knows when to keep absolutely quiet. And to put the kettle on.

PAM BROWN

August 8

Our affections
are our life.
We live by them;
they supply
our warmth.

WILLIAM ELLERY CHANNING
(1780-1842)

May 28

Beauty, truth, friendship, love, creation – these are the great values of life. We can't prove them, or explain them, yet they are the most stable things in our lives.

DR. JESSE HERMAN HOLMES

August 7

...in the sweetness of friendship
let there be laughter,
and sharing of pleasures...
the heart finds its morning
and is refreshed.

KAHLIL GIBRAN (1883-1931), FROM "THE PROPHET"

May 29

Friendship is based on
chemistry and trust...
and why it happens or why
it rises and falls, and rises
again, is a mystery,
like a fine piece of music.

RICHARD LOUV, FROM "THE WEB OF LIFE"

August 6

We can never replace
a friend. When we are
fortunate enough to have
several, we find they are all
different. No one has
a double in friendship.

JOHANN SCHILLER (1759-1805)

May 30

Everyone must have felt that a cheerful friend is like a sunny day, which sheds its brightness on all around.

SIR J. LUBBOCK (1834-1913)

August 5

And I will remember you.
Crying, singing, laughing.
Always there. Always kind.
My friend through all my problems.

JANE SWAN, B.1943

The need for friendship is as deep
as the need for food.

JOSHUA LIEBMAN

August 4

To have a good friend is one of
the highest delights of life;
to be a good friend is one of life's most
difficult and rewarding undertakings.

FROM "SHARE THE HOPE"

The only way
to multiply happiness
is to divide it.

PAUL SCHERER

August 3

You like to hear about the ordinary things in my life. Just because it's me. I'm very grateful – you're a great audience!

MARION C. GARRETTY
(1917-2005)

June 2

Trouble is a sieve through which
we sift our acquaintances.
Those too big to pass through
are our friends.

ARLENE FRANCIS (1907-2001)

August 2

Friendship... does not abolish distance between human beings but brings that distance to life.

WALTER BENJAMIN

June 3

We have been friends together in sunshine and in shade.

CAROLINE NORTON (1808-1877)

August 1

Do not keep the alabaster boxes of your love and tenderness sealed up until your friends are dead. Fill their lives with sweetness. Speak approving cheering words while their ears can hear them and while their hearts can be thrilled by them.

GEORGE W. CHILDS (1829-1894)

The truth in friendship
is to me every bit as sacred
as eternal marriage.

KATHERINE MANSFIELD (1888-1923)

I can let my hair down, forget about how I'm dressed and feel completely relaxed with you. I hope I can give that back to you too.

MARION C. GARRETTY
(1917-2005)

Friendships multiply joys
and divide griefs.

PROVERB

Friends are true twins in soul;
they sympathise in everything.

WILLIAM PENN (1644-1718)

June 6

We need friendship all the time, just as much as we need the proverbial prime necessities of life, fire and water.

CICERO (106-43 B.C.)

Do not save your loving speeches for your friends till they are dead; do not write them on their tombstones, speak them rather now instead.

ANNA CUMMINS

You believe in me.
There are no trite words of thanks that
could tell you what that means to me.

INGEBORG NELSON

July 28

When people laugh at their troubles they lose a good many friends. Friends never forgive the loss of their prerogative.

H. L. MENCKEN (1880-1956)

June 8

A friend is the person
who in a mechanical emergency
always asks you, very gently,
whether you've switched
the thing on!

PAM BROWN

Life is not worth living
for the person
who has not even one
good friend.

DEMOCRITUS OF ABDERA
(5TH-4TH CENTURY B.C.)

June 9

My Friend:
In prosperity a pleasure,
a solace in adversity,
in grief a comfort,
in joy a merry companion,
at all times an other I.

JOHN LYLY (1544-1606)

A person is a knot,
a web, a mesh into which
relationships are tied.
Only those relationships
matter.

ANTOINE DE SAINT-EXUPERY (1900-1944)

June 10

True friendship is like sound health, the value of it is seldom known until it be lost.

CHARLES CALEB COLTON (1780-1832)

The only rose without thorns
is friendship.

MADELINE DE SCUDERY

June 11

Oh the comfort, the inexpressible comfort of feeling safe with a person; having neither to weigh thoughts nor measure words, but to pour them out. Just as they are, chaff and grain together.

DINAH MARIA MULOCK CRAIK (1826-1887),
FROM "A LIFE FOR A LIFE"

Lifelong friends give.
They give a lifetime. You do.
And "thank you"
will never be enough.

HELEN EXLEY

My friend!
You yourself are my treasure,
The chain of gold around my neck.

BENGALI FOLK SONG

Hast thou a friend?
Visit her often,
for thorns and brushwood
obstruct the road
which no one treads.

EASTERN PROVERB

June 13

You're a special friend.
For your deep kindness, great thanks.

HELEN FITZWALTER-READ

In Gujerati, which is my mother tongue, we have a word "Lehnoo" which is almost impossible to translate into English. The nearest equivalent would be a combination of attraction and affinity of spirit...

NADIR DINSHAW

Part of what friends experience is something that people who aren't friends can't know. It's a code. It's another language.

JUDD NELSON

July 21

...friendship only is, indeed, genuine when two friends, without speaking a word to each other, can, nevertheless, find happiness in being together.

GEORG EBERS (1837-1898)

Friendship is our most precious possession. More valuable than gold. It is crucial that time is taken to develop friendships even if this means sacrificing wealth. For without friendship life becomes merely an existence.

STUART AND LINDA MACFARLANE

July 20

The friends are closest to us who best understand what life means to us, who feel for us as we feel for ourselves, who are bound to us in triumph and disaster, who break the spell of our loneliness.

HENRY ALONZO MYERS

Friendship is always a sweet responsibility, never an opportunity.

KAHLIL GIBRAN (1883-1931)

July 19

Nothing can come between
true friends.

EURIPIDES (484-406 B.C.)

Friends choose each other, try each other out, don't have to go too fast at first, don't have to promise to have lunch every day from now to eternity.

MARGARET MEAD (1901-1978)

July 18

A day for toil, an hour for sport,
but for a friend is life too short.

RALPH WALDO EMERSON (1803-1882)

June 18

Seeing a good friend is like going home,
or like tasting Mother's cooking.
I feel secure, and need not protect myself.
"Here," I say, "it is safe."

ARNOLD R. BEISSER (1925-1991)

Your friend is the antidote to despair,
the elixir of hope, the tonic
for depression... Give to that friend
without reluctance.

AUTHOR UNKNOWN

Surely there's something more impressive in the dictionary than a lame "thank you"! It doesn't begin to express what I feel about you, the support you've been to me.

MARGOT THOMSON

July 16

There is nothing we like to see so much as the gleam of pleasure in a person's eye when they feel that we have sympathized, understood, interested ourself in their welfare. These moments are the moments worth living.

DON MARQUIS, FROM "PREFACES"

June 20

A friend you've had since school-days
shares memories no one else can.
Part of you both is still ten years old.

PAMELA DUGDALE

A million billion words
have been spoken about
what friendship means,
but two good friends
can be together without
speaking a single word
and know precisely what
friendship means.

STUART AND LINDA MACFARLANE

June 21

Friend, whatever hardships
threaten,
If you call me,
I'll befriend you,
All-enduring, fearlessly,
I'll befriend you.

OGLALA SIOUX INDIAN

Friendship serves a great host of
different purposes all at the same time.
In whatever direction you turn,
it still remains yours.
No barrier can shut it out.
It can never be untimely;
it can never be in the way.

CICERO (106-43 B.C.)

June 22

The finest ship to sail the sea of life
is Friendship.

J.M. ROBERTSON

Thank you that you are,
Thank you for just being.

HELEN THOMSON

June 23

I've told the same story around
thirty-nine times.
You looked intrigued,
you laughed thirty-nine times.
That's been one of your gifts
to me.

HELEN EXLEY

We cannot really love anybody with whom we never laugh.

AGNES REPPLIER (1855-1950)

June24

The mind is rarely so disturbed but that the company of a friend will restore it to some degree of tranquility and sedateness.

ADAM SMITH (1723-1790)

July 11

When anything sensational
happens my first instinct
is to phone you.
Thank heavens I like you
enough to wait till morning.
Usually.

PAM BROWN

Next to goodness itself,
I entreat you to regard friendship
as the finest thing in all the world.

LAELIUS

Fate gives us parents;
choice gives us friends.

FROM "PROSIT: A BOOK OF TOASTS"

We are not friends
because of the laughs
we spend
but the tears we save.

NIKKI GIOVANNI

July 9

Your friend is the one who knows all about you, and still likes you.

ELBERT HUBBARD (1856-1915)

June27

When a friend asks
there is no tomorrow.

GEORGE HERBERT (1593-1633)

Love and friendship
are the discoveries of ourselves
in others, and our delight in
the recognition.

ALEXANDER SMITH (1830-1867)

June 28

A friend is one who steps in when all the world has gone out.

ENTRY IN AN AUTOGRAPH ALBUM

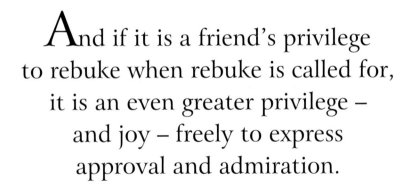

And if it is a friend's privilege
to rebuke when rebuke is called for,
it is an even greater privilege –
and joy – freely to express
approval and admiration.

GERTRUDE BUCKMAN

Once established, friendship
is a simple pleasure, a place
where we can be ourselves
without weighing our words
or watching our manners.

MICHELLE LOVRIC

Life is partly what we make it,
and partly what it is made
by the friends whom we choose.

TEHYI HSIEH

A friend hath the skill and observation of the best physician; the diligence and vigilance of the best nurse; and the tenderness and patience of the best mother.

EDWARD HYDE, LORD CLARENDON (1609-1674)

July 5

A friend may well be reckoned the masterpiece of nature.

RALPH WALDO EMERSON (1803-1882)

July 1

Friendship cheers like a sunbeam;
charms like a good story;
inspires like a brave leader;
binds like a golden chain.

NEWELL D. HILLIS

It's just the little homely things,
The unobtrusive, friendly things,
The "Won't-you-let-me-help-you" things...
That make the world seem bright.

AUTHOR UNKNOWN

There is no desire
so deep as the simple desire
for companionship.

GRAHAM GREENE (1904-1991)

July 3

...the language of friendship,
love and care doesn't change.

FROM "THE FRIENDSHIP BOOK OF FRANCIS GAY"